For Raphaël and Louise

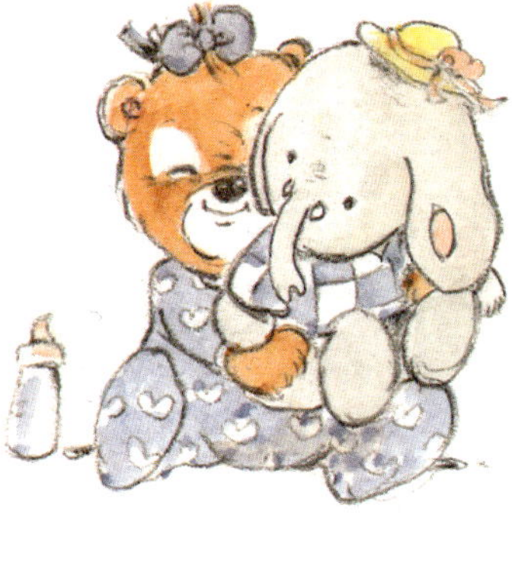

He's My Elephant!

Claude K Dubois

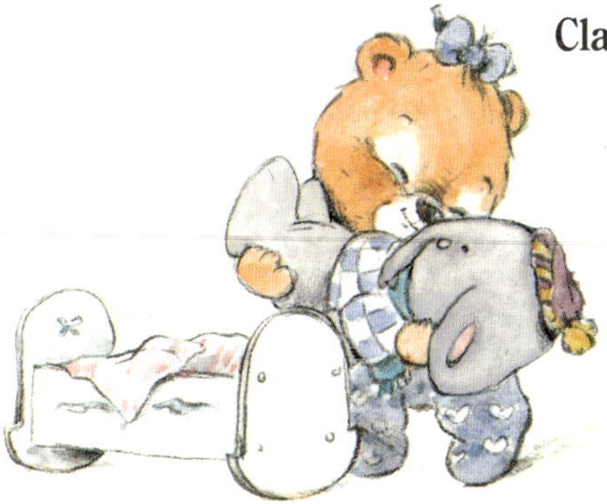

He's My Elephant!

Claude K Dubois

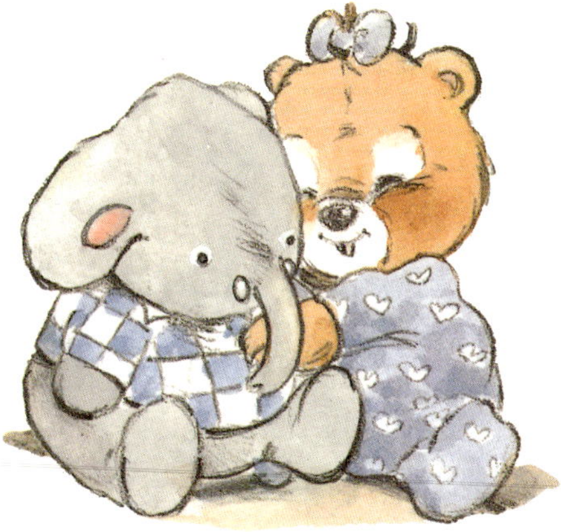

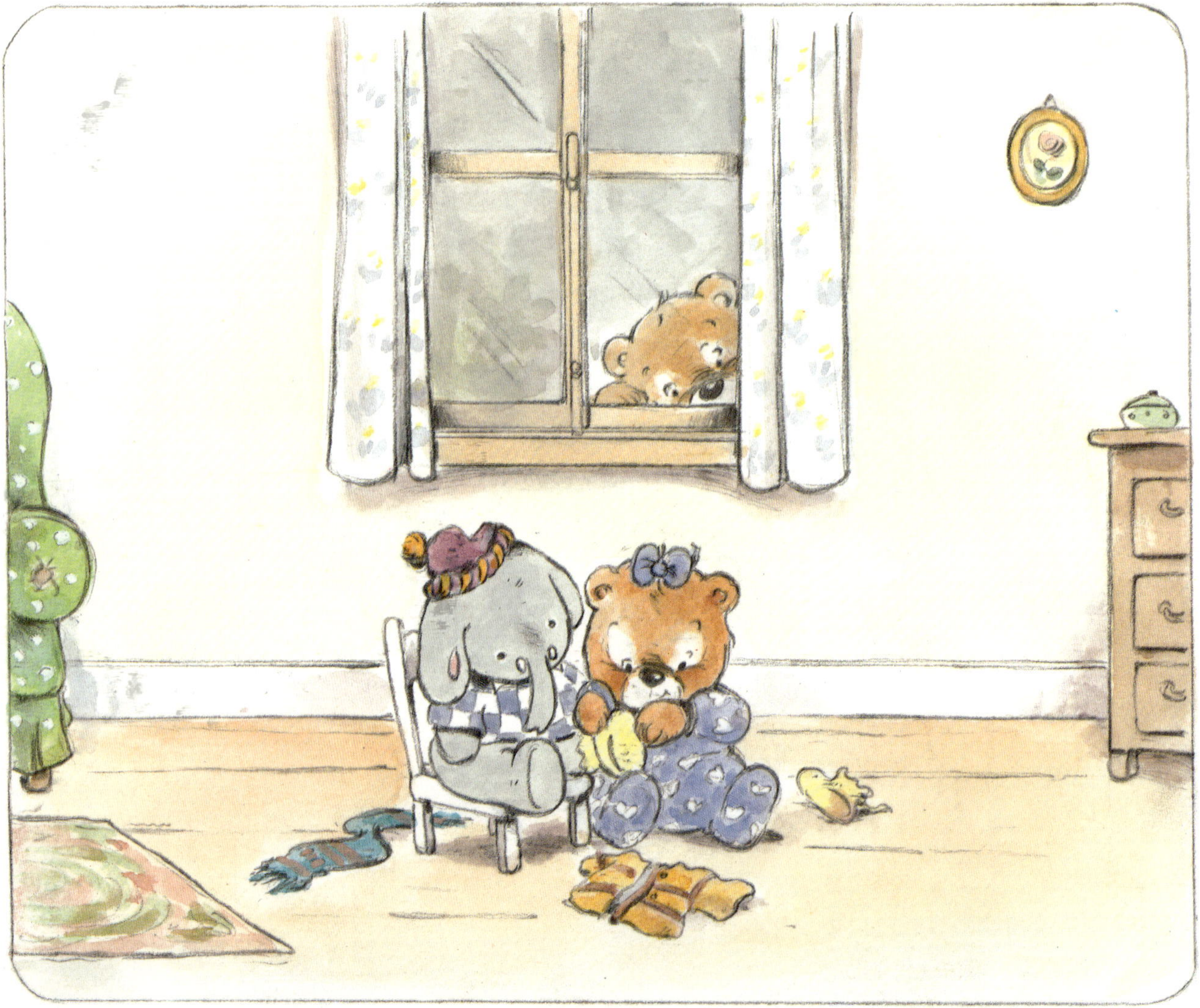

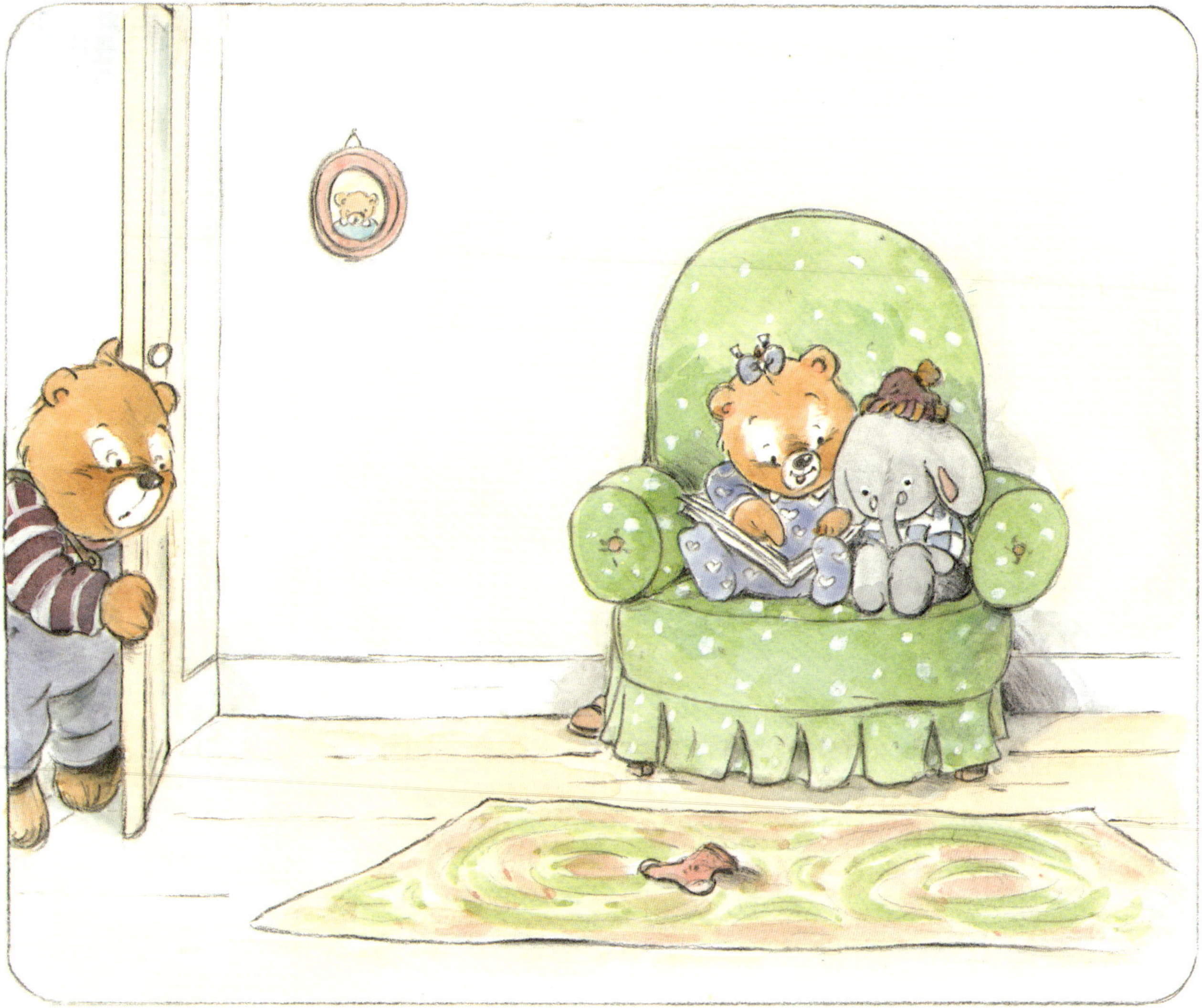

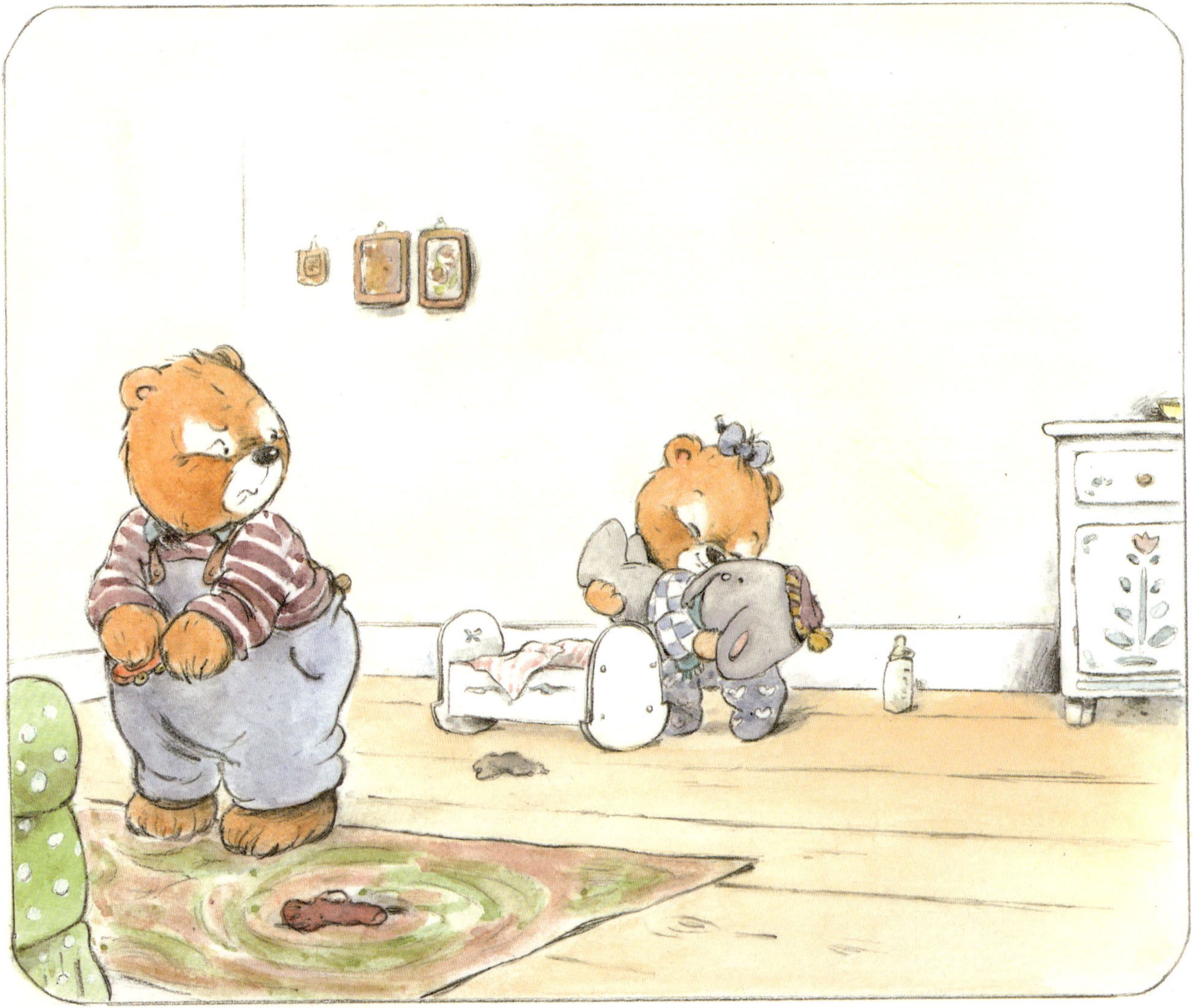

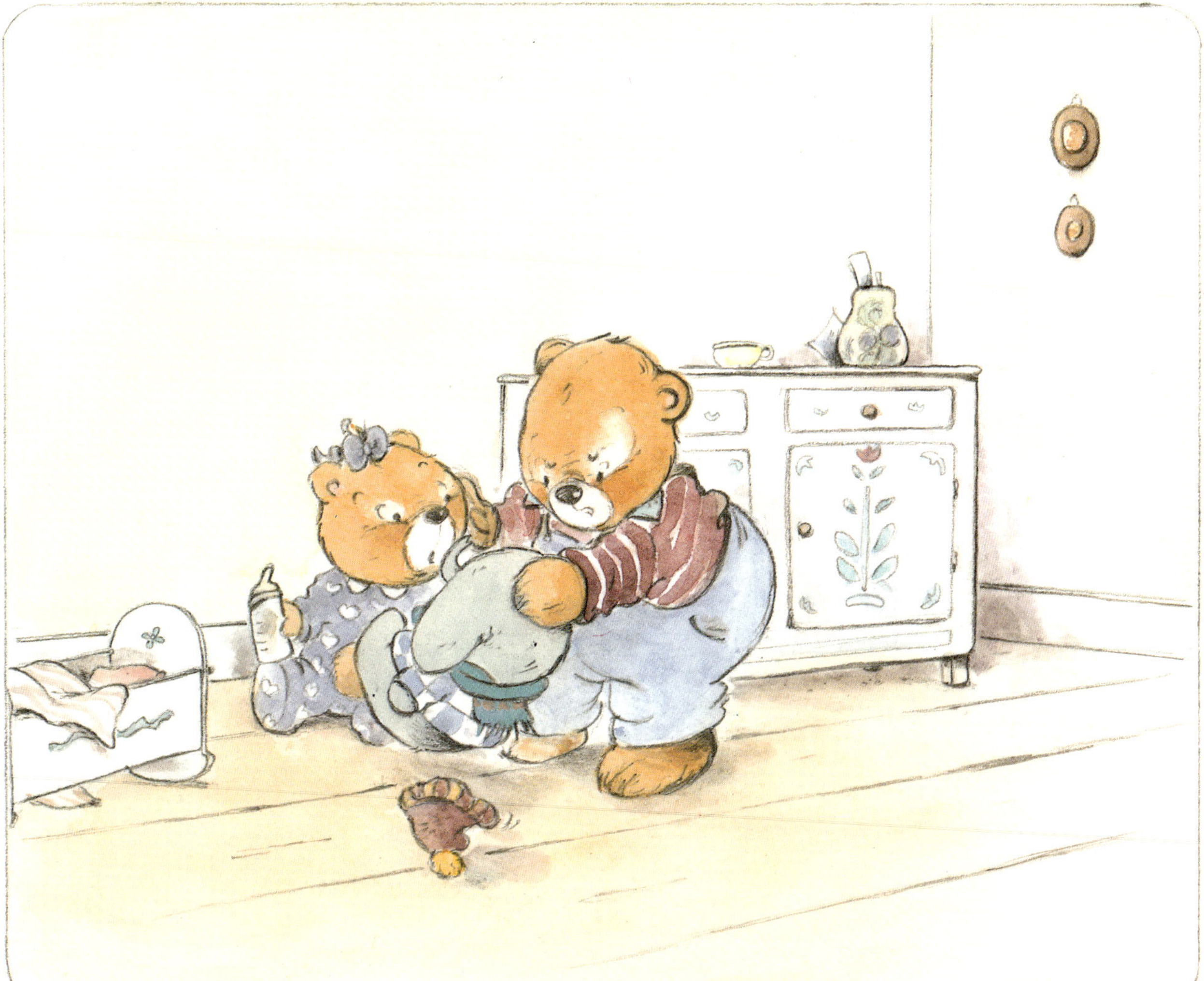

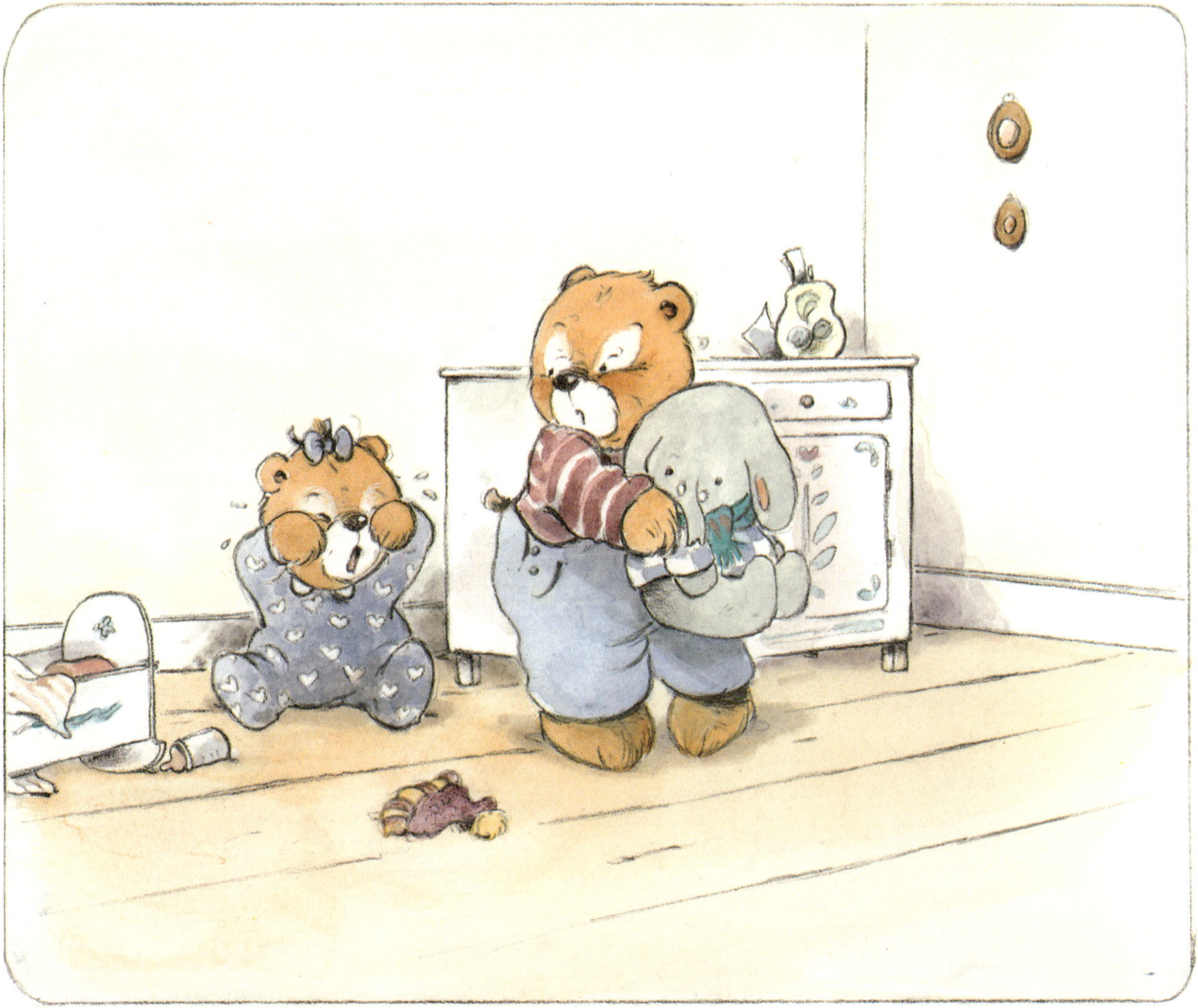

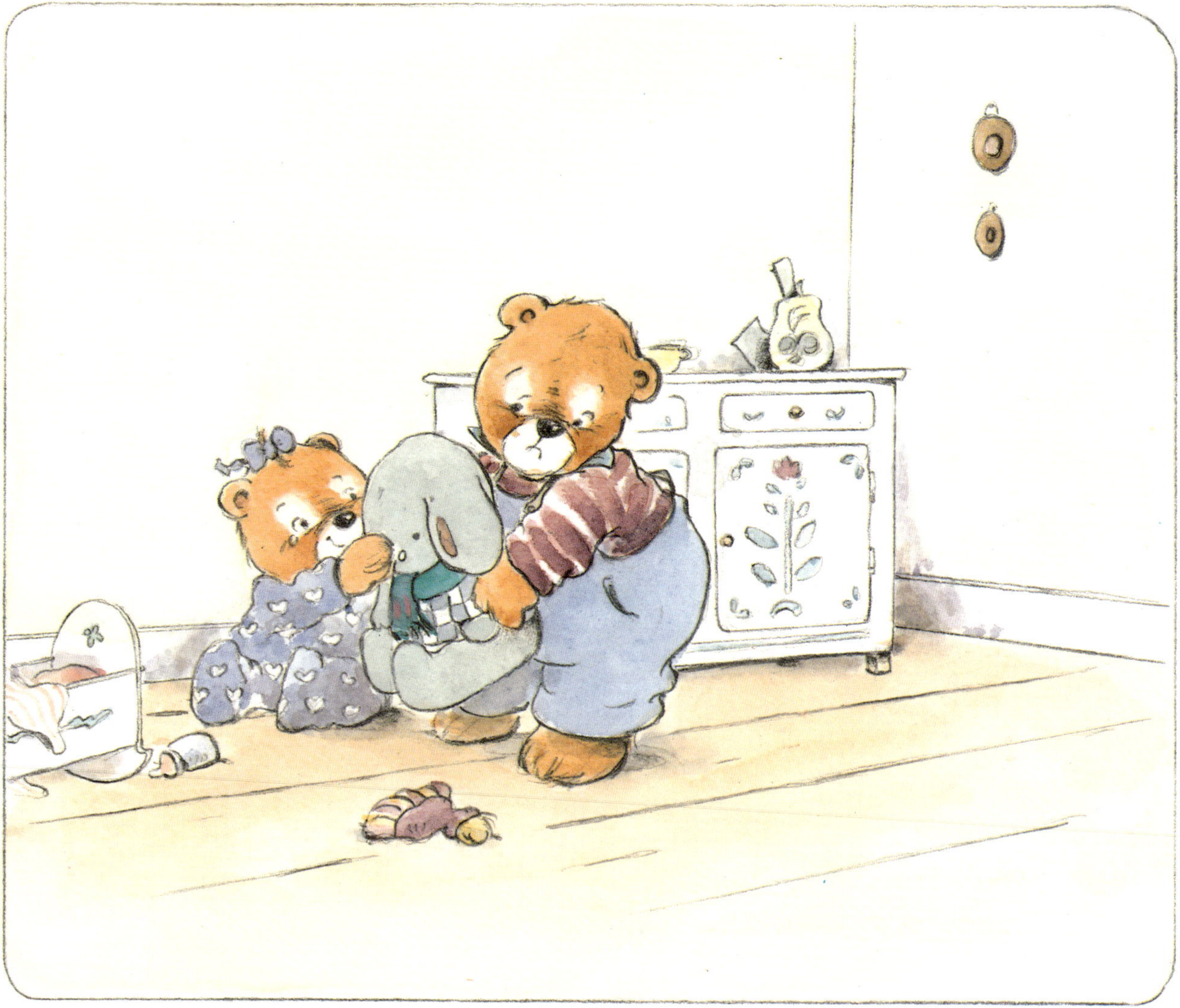

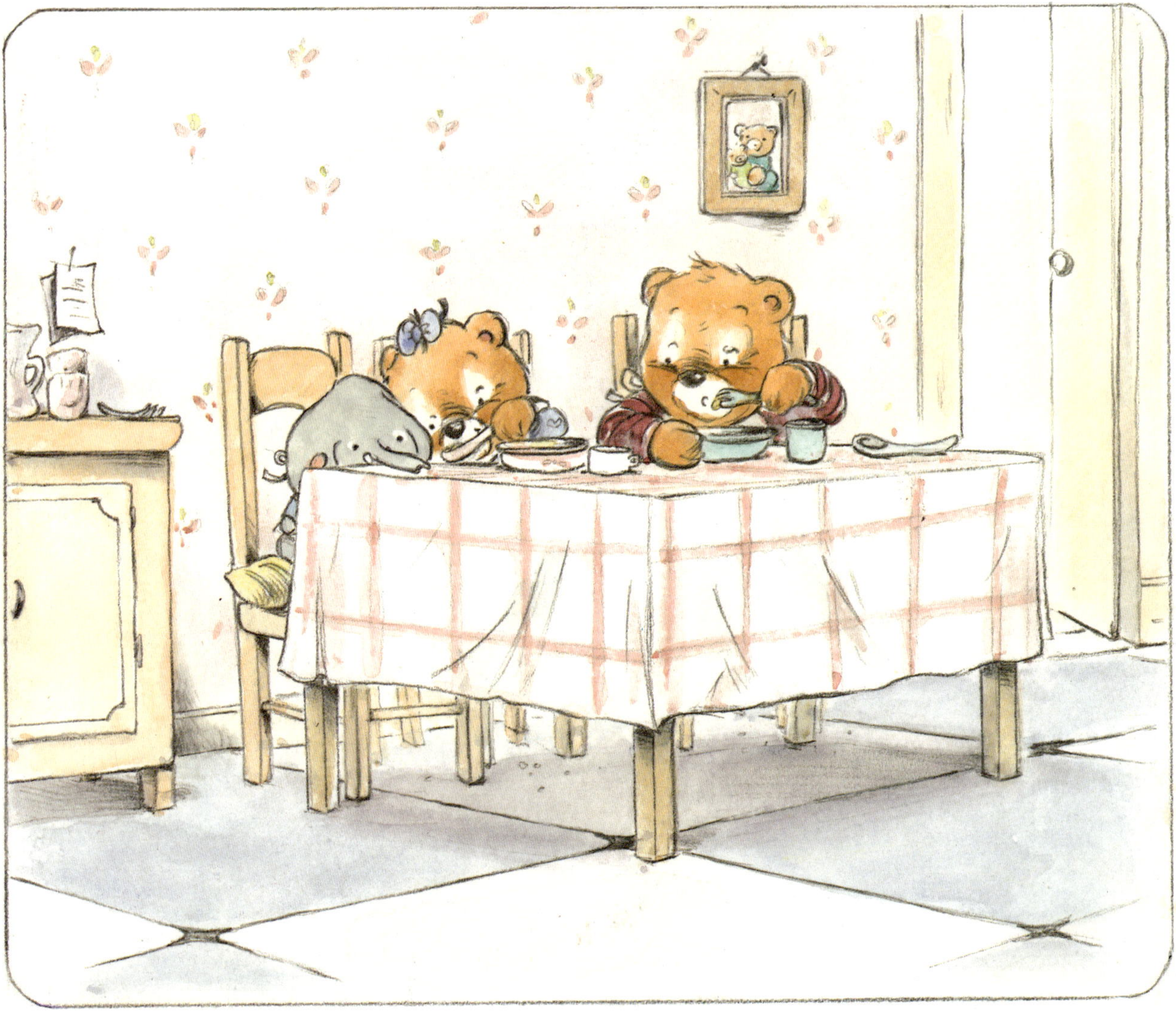

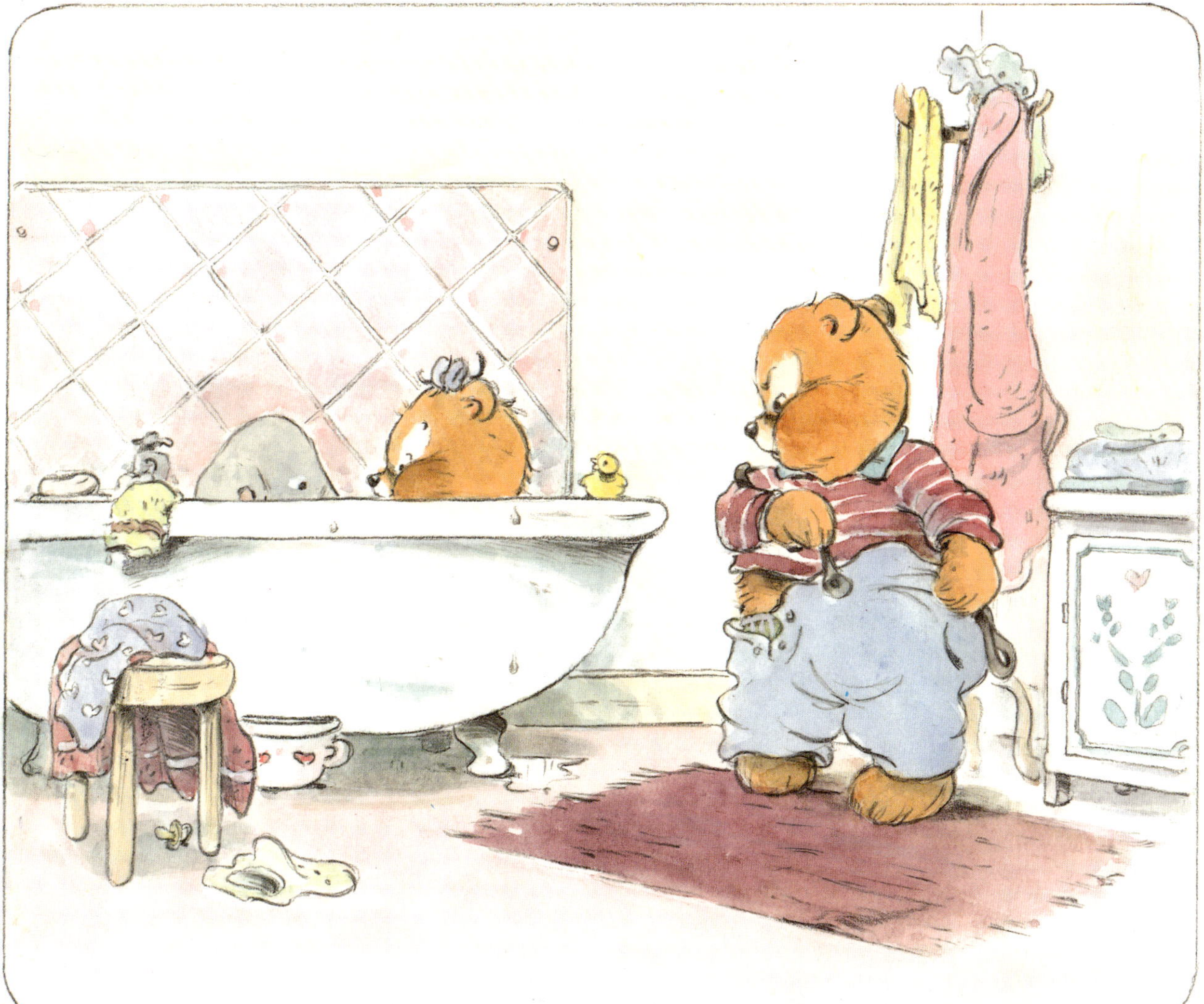

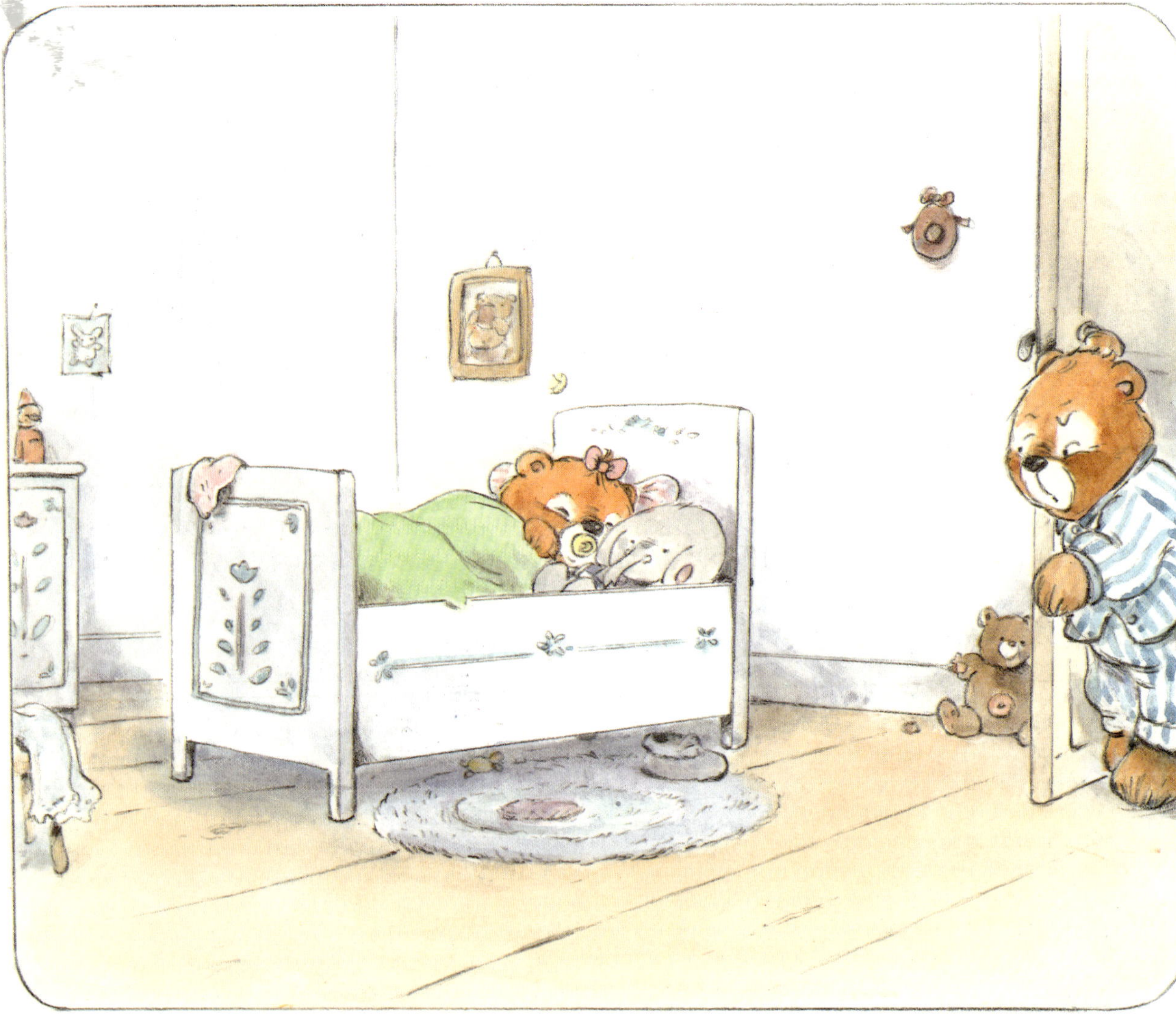

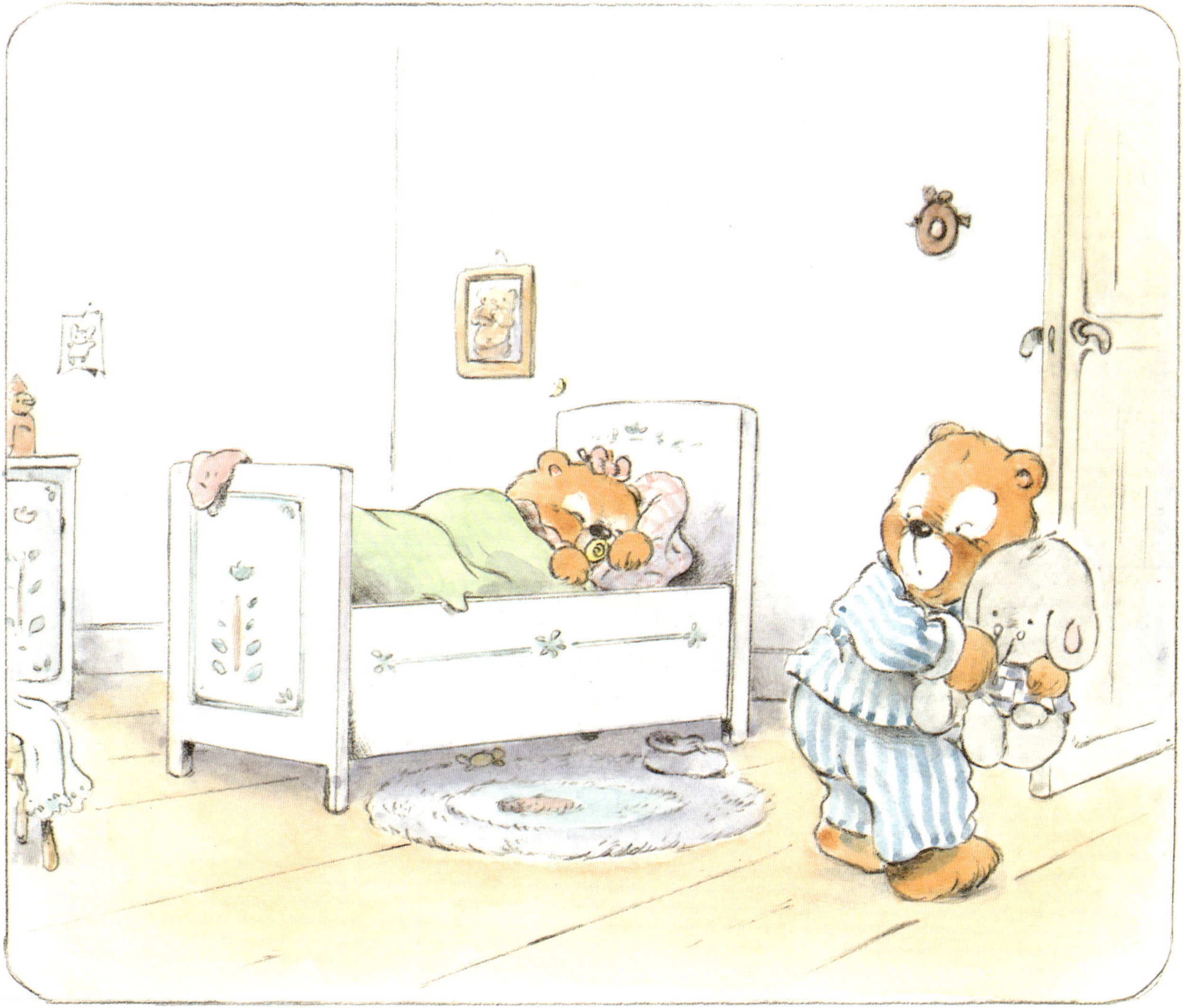

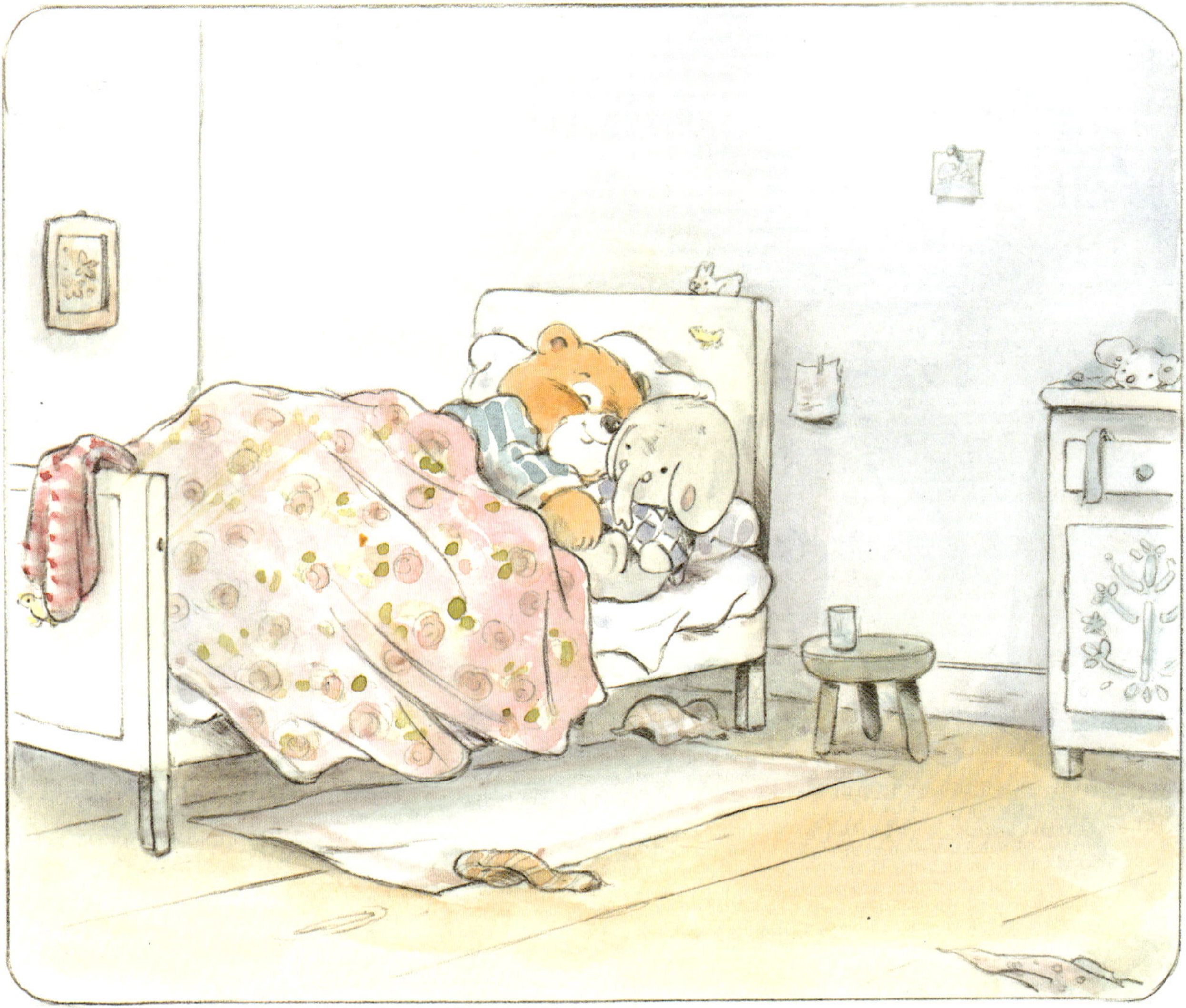

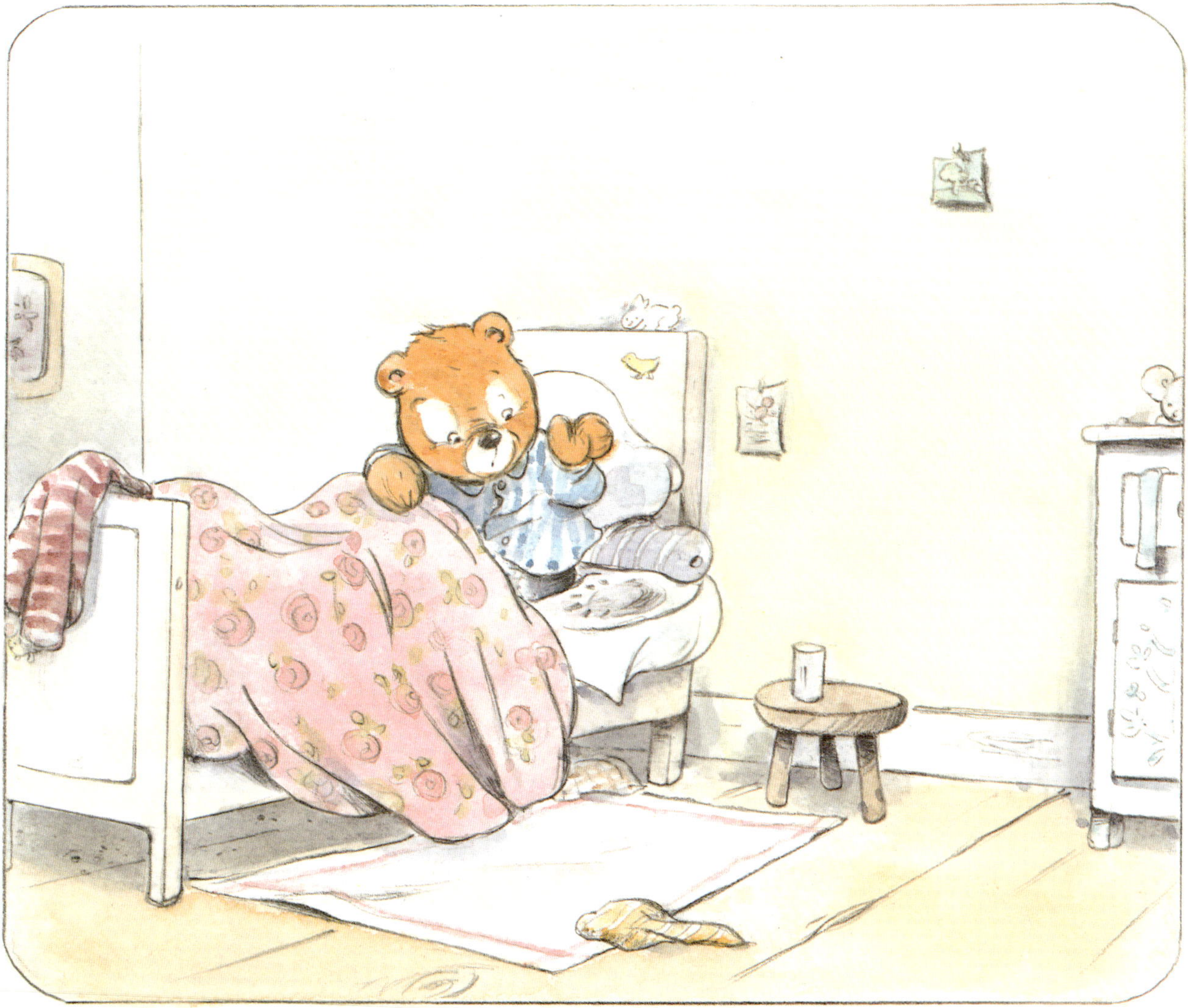

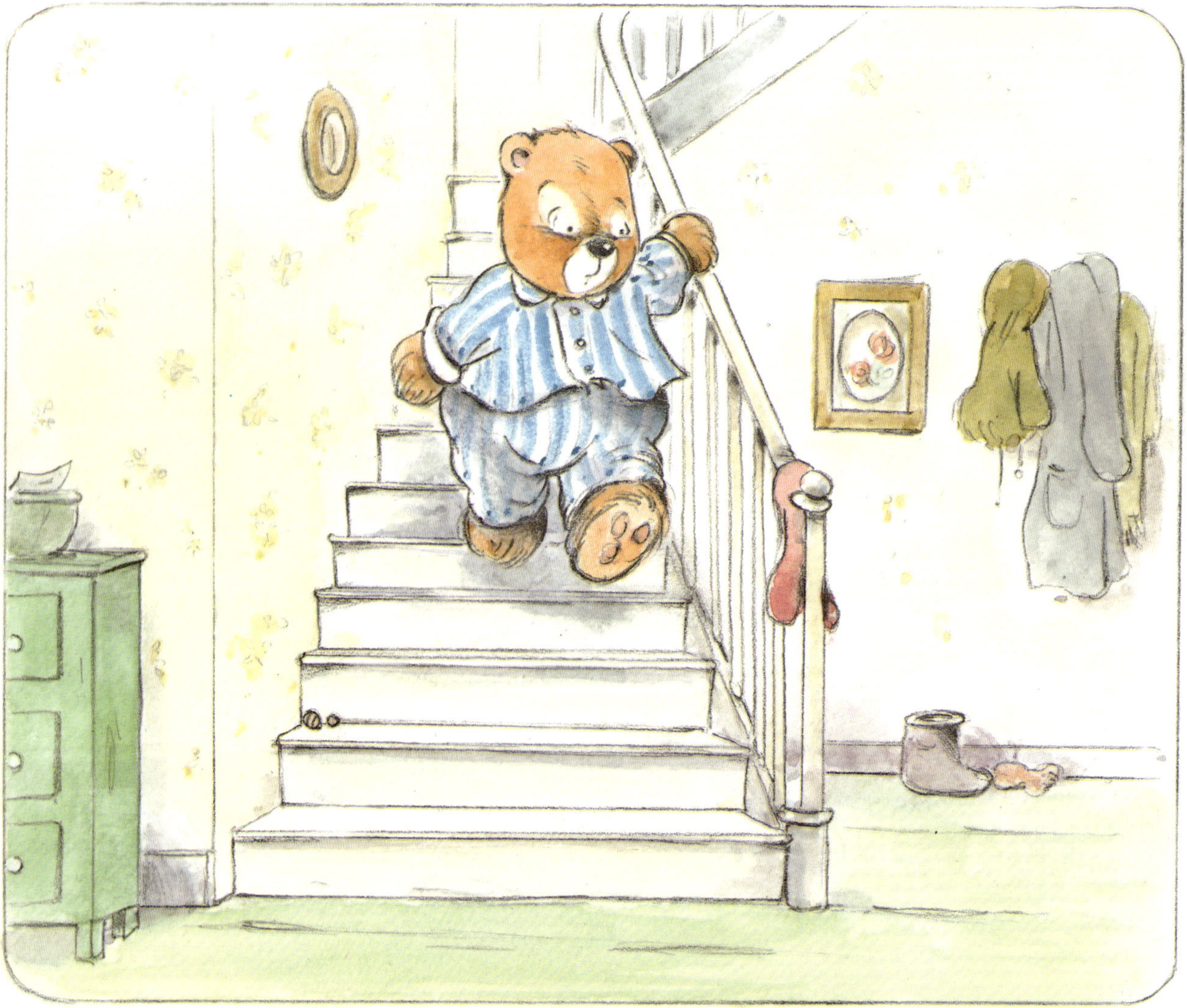

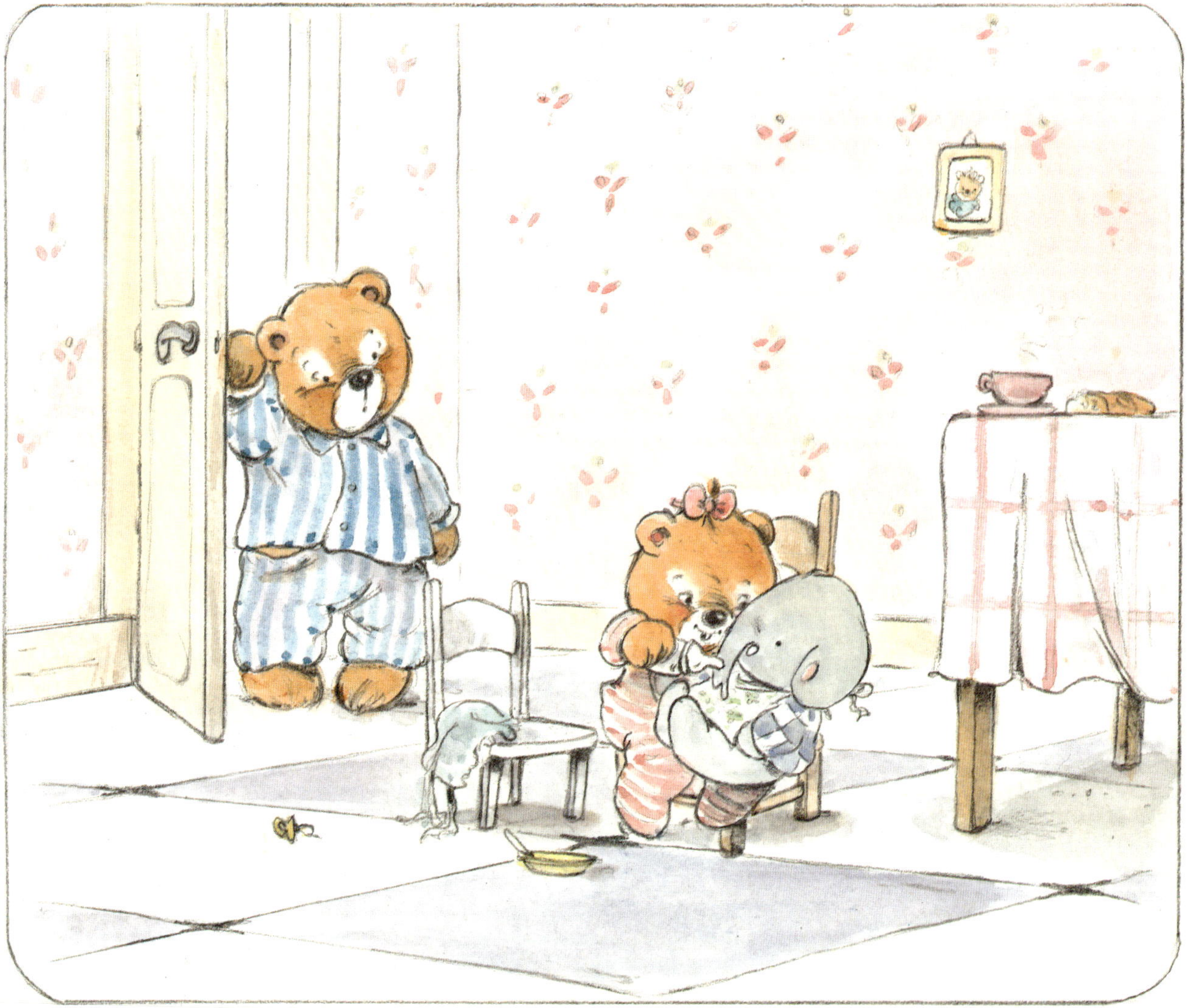

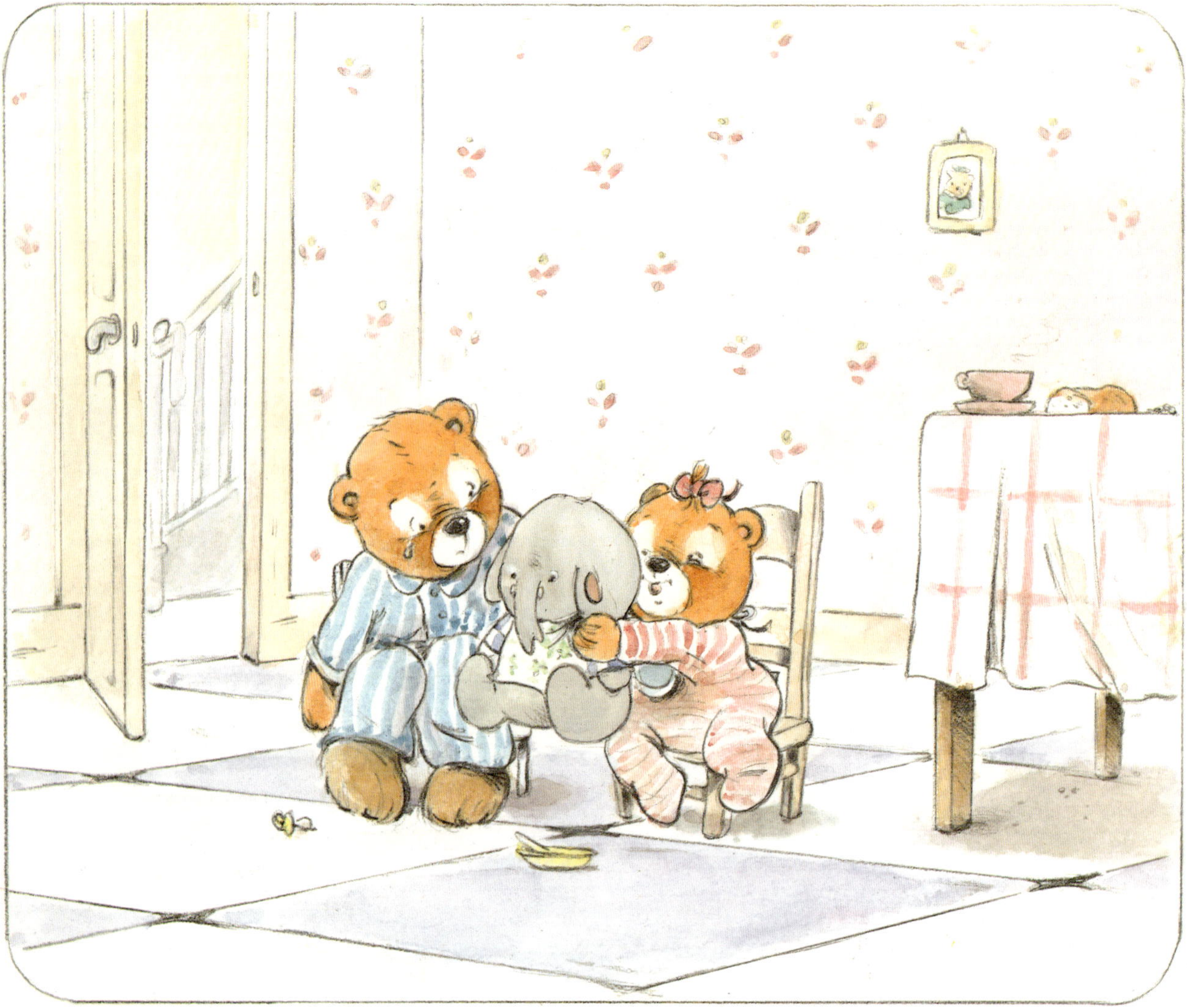

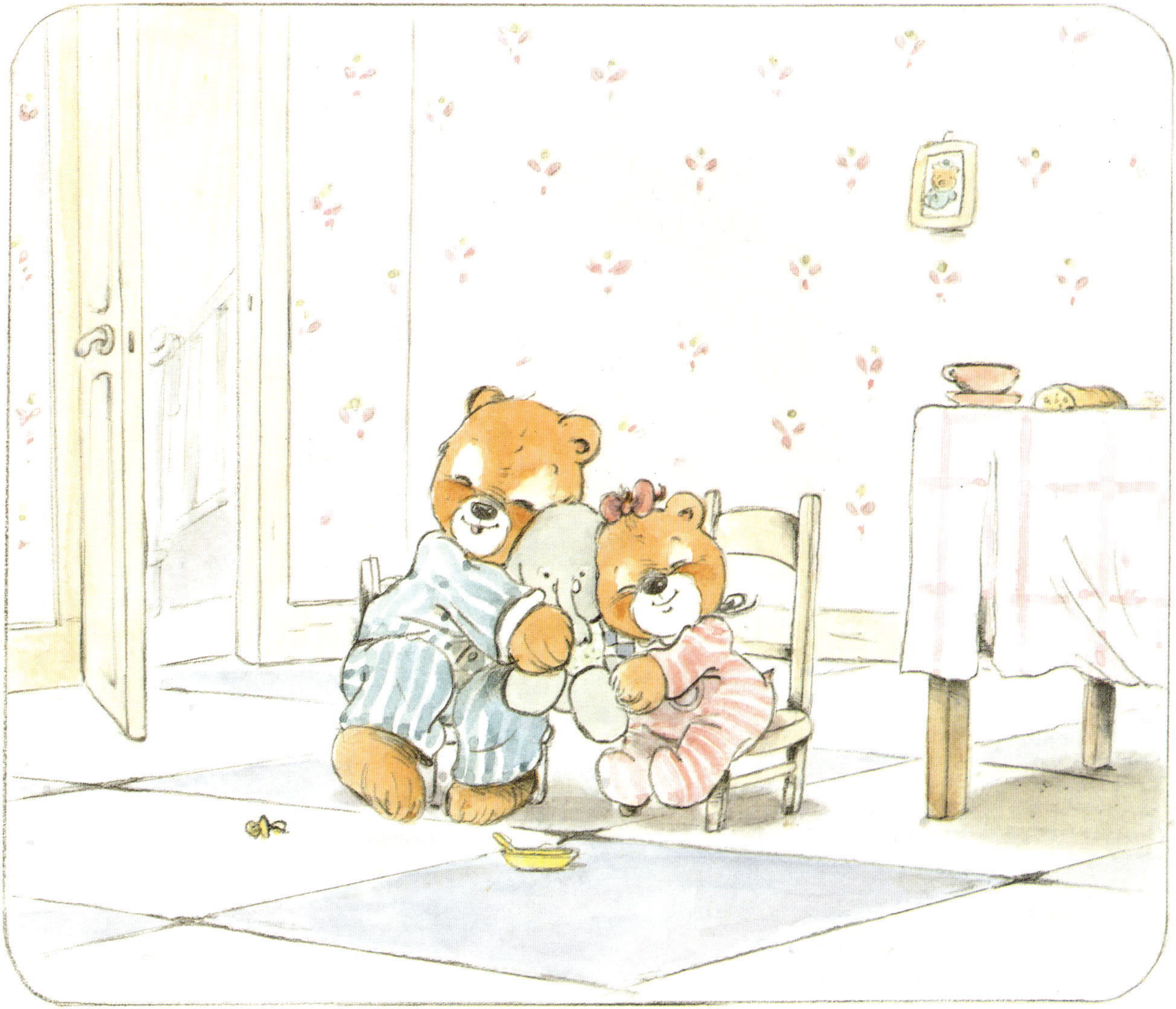

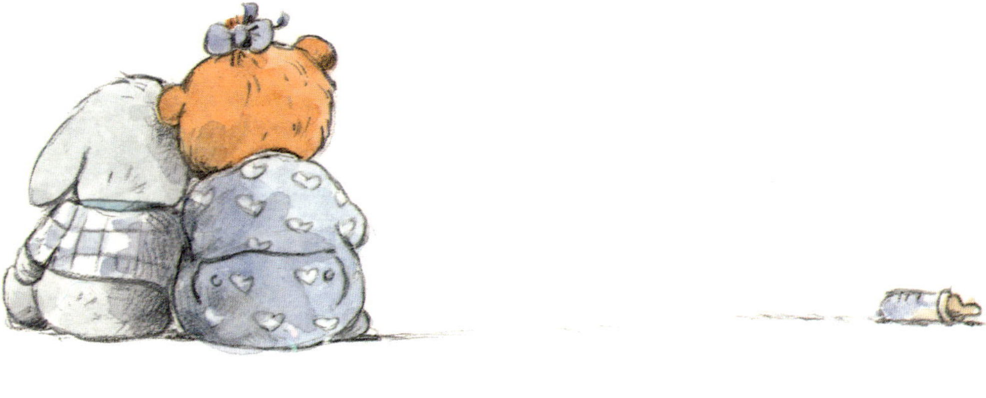